J. Ogilvie

A Proposal for Liquidating 66,666,666 2 3

Of the Three per Cents, by Converting the Land Tax into a...

J. Ogilvie

A Proposal for Liquidating 66,666,666 2 3
Of the Three per Cents, by Converting the Land Tax into a...

ISBN/EAN: 9783337151478

Printed in Europe, USA, Canada, Australia, Japan

Cover: Foto ©Paul-Georg Meister /pixelio.de

More available books at **www.hansebooks.com**

A
PROPOSAL

FOR

LIQUIDÂTING 66,666,666$\frac{2}{3}$

OF THE

THREE PER CENTS,

&c. &c.

PROPOSAL

FOR LIQUIDATING

66,666,666

OF THE

THREE PER CENTS,

BY

CONVERTING THE LAND TAX

INTO A

PERMANENT ANNUITY;

WITH

CURSORY OBSERVATIONS.

Humbly fubmitted to

BOTH HOUSES OF PARLIAMENT.

There is a tide in the affairs of men,
Which, taken at the flood, leads on to fortune:
Omitted, all the voyage of their life
Is bound in fhallows and in miferies.   SHAKESPEARE.

LONDON:

PRINTED FOR J. WRIGHT, OPPOSITE OLD BOND STREET,
PICCADILLY.

1798.

LET it be remembered, that from the wife and benevolent order of our nature every fituation has, together with its difadvantages, certain relative advantages; which can, not only afford fome alleviation to the greateft diftrefs, but which, if timely feized and judicioufly improved, may throw a ray of light on the moft gloomy appearances, and open fairer fcenes and brighter profpects to the active and intelligent mind.

With this view, I feel an inclination rather to confider the prefent ftate of public credit as ftill poffefling fources of hope; than to indulge in melancholy defcriptions, which are not only ufelefs, but which, by exciting alarms and apprehenfions, have a direct tendency to augment our diftrefs, and to incapacitate us from reaping the benefit of the refources we ftill poffefs.

Our fituation, it muft be confeffed, is far from being pleafant, and our profpects from being cheerful. Nay, whatever gloomy apprehenfions

B   were

were entertained towards the clofe of the American war, apply, with additional force, to the prefent moment. But political difcuffions being foreign to my prefent objeƈt, I fhall not ftop to inquire by what caufes we have been brought into this fituation, nor by what means we are beft to get out of it: leaving thefe weighty difcuffions to thofe who are better qualified for the arduous inquiry, I profefs my fole aim to be, to contribute my endeavours to point out the means of fupporting us under the fituation fuch as I have defcribed it ; and of enabling us to provide for the great expenfe incident to a period of preffure and embarraffment.

If the land proprietor fhould be ftartled at the firft propofition of felling the land tax, let him paufe a moment, and attentively perufe my *Propofal*; in which I flatter myfelf he will find nothing to frighten or to difpleafe him, and a great deal to raife his fpirits, and to give him a better opinion of the fafety of the ftate than he entertained before. Let him carry in his mind to the perufal, that the 3 *per cents*, which, before the war, were above 96, are now about 49, little more than one half of their former value ; that all hopes of peace for this year are vanifhed ; that fupplies muft be raifed for an aƈtive, vigorous, and defperate campaign; that it is impoffible to raife the neceffary fupplies in the ordinary way, by loan,

while

while ftocks are fo low ; and that extraordinary means muft be reforted to.

From the prefent amount of the national debt, without taking into confideration the increafe that muft follow from the continuance of the war, I believe that there is not a land proprietor in the kingdom who expects that in his life time the land tax ever can be lefs than four fhillings in the pound ; and my *Propofal* goes not to a forced fale, but barely to the application of what may be confidered as already permanent—trufting that by judicious management, this valuable fund may be applied fo as to prevent greater diftrefs and heavier burdens; to revive, animate, and invigorate public credit ; and to open the means for raifing the fupplies requifite for two years; if the obftinacy of the conteft fhould fo long prevent mankind from returning to the bleffings of peace.

I have faid above, that it is impoffible to raife the neceffary fupplies in the ordinary way, by loan—I fhould have added, without difcovering fome means of raifing the ftocks from their prefent ftate of depreffion. Should 25 millions only be wanted, fuch a loan would probably fink the 3 *per cents* to from 45 to 40, which would be funding from 45 to 62 millions for 25. Such a meafure, if not impoffible, muft be admitted to be ruinous, and would defeat the moft flattering prof-

pects

peêts that the prefent afpeê of the *finking fund* prefents to the holders of ftock.

Under thefe circumftances, the public have very generally turned their eyes towards the *land tax;* as hoping, fome way or other, to be able to convert it into a refource for raifing the fupplies for the fervice of the enfuing year; though I have never heard any praêicable mode by which that meafure was to be effeêed, that was not liable to very ftrong objeêions.

Before I proceed to confider the mode generally recommended, I would beg leave to obferve that the land tax is already virtually pledged to the public creditor; and that it can neither be fold nor mortgaged without replacing it by an equivalent; and even, with the moft unexceptionable equivalent that could be propofed, that there would be confiderabte danger of fhaking public credit, and deprefling the funds ftill more, by withdrawing what the ftock holder confiders, at prefent, as his beft fecurity; for, though the land tax be voted annually, long prefcription has rated it as *permanent,* and the vote is confidered as matter of form.

I would farther beg leave to make one other general obfervation. I have frequently heard a fpeculative opinion, of a very dangerous nature, fupported with apparent plaufibility; that a public bankruptcy

bankruptcy, though it would fall heavy on individuals, would be the means of enriching the ftate; that the public, by getting rid of the old, would begin a new fcore, and would find refources for half, a century in the ruin of the exifting fyftem of finance. But he who argues in this manner is precisely the boy in the fable, who killed the goofe that laid golden eggs. In his avaricious ignorance, he would deftroy the very mine from whence the ftate derives her chief fupply. Deftroy the national debt, and you abolifh a fund of near 16 millions a year, which is now applicable to the fervice of the ftate. Taxation is undoubtedly a grievous burden; but in war, it is alfo the fource of fupplies. Stop the one, you deftroy the other for a time.—That there are many and great inconveniencies arifing from the prefent fyftem, is perfectly true; and it fhould be the firft object of an enlightened adminiftration to devife the means to correct and alleviate them.

What might be the comparative merit of a new order of things that muft be produced by a diffolution of the prefent fyftem, I cannot pretend even to guefs; but if fuddenly produced, it would be a fyftem diftinct from a monied intereft, and incompatible with the fupplies abfolutely neceffary under the prefent ftate of things; and at all events,

the

the tranſition would be a frightful period of general deſtruction, which would, in all probability, involve *Prerogative, Privilege,* and *Property,* in
one common ruin. They all, in my opinion, reſt
on the baſis of public credit ; and one common
fate awaits them all.

· If the land Proprietor is weak enough to ima-
gine that he would be exempt from the conſe-
quences of a general derangement of the monied
intereſt, he is equally miſtaken : the land, indeed,
is fixed, but the Proprietor is moveable. But even
if no ſuch danger awaited them, the ruin of *public
credit,* and failure of the funded ſyſtem, would of
itſelf, by raiſing the price of money, reduce their
nominal rentals very conſiderably ; which, for a
long time, would be a ſource of many and great
inconveniencies. So that, abſtracted from the obli-
gations of good faith, and the dangers to be juſtly
apprehended from a convulſion, the landed intereſt is particularly and immediately involved with
the monied intereſt, and embarked in one common
bottom. Their cauſe is common, and their fate
will be the ſame.

The only mode of applying the land tax to the
ſervice of the enſuing year that I have heard of, is
either by ſelling it to the land owner, or to the
higheſt bidder by contract, in the ordinary courſe

of

of a loan; both presupposing that the land tax should be made perpetual.

If the first were practicable, the interest of the proprietors would be better consulted, and the transaction would have a more equitable appearance : but as time would be requisite to complete the purchase, it is evident that it could not be depended on for furnishing the supplies for the service of the ensuing year. It remains then only to carry it to market, and supposing that the two millions land tax were appropriated to pay the interest of the specific sums to be raised on them, and allowing that the nature of the security should give it an advantage of 5 *per cent.* over any other stock of the same rate ; I very much question whether, considering the present price of money, a loan of 25 or 30 millions could be raised on this fund, much above 53, 64, and 75, in the 3, 4, and 5 *per cents.* But allowing that the whole could be had on a 5 *per cent.* stock as high as 80, the two millions land tax would raise only 32 millions, little more than the supply neceffary for one year.

And the great objection of shaking public credit, by a *separate appropriation* of the land tax, would still remain : nor would there, in this measure, be any thing found to counteract the farther depreffion of the funds, which the addition of
debt,

debt, exclufive of the circumftance of weakening
the fecurity, is alone calculated to produce.

In the following Propofal, I have had it particularly in view to guard againft the above objection;
while the mode of application that I am about to
recommend will have the direct tendency not only
to *raife the funds* very confiderably at prefent, but
alfo to prevent them from falling hereafter to their
prefent low ftate. With this view I would propofe—

———————

1ft. That the land tax at the rate of four fhillings in the pound, producing two millions a year,
fhould be made perpetual, and declared the firft
lien on every refpective eftate.

2d. That thefe two millions fhould be converted into a government annuity—under the name
of the *land tax annuity.*

3d. That each land holder fhould have an exclufive privilege of redeeming his *own* land tax,
or purchafing a fhare of the land tax annuity
equal to it, at 25 years purchafe.

4th. That the redemption price fhould be paid
to government in 3 *per cent.* ftock, which fhould
be received at 75.

5th. The price of the 3 *per cents* being admitted at 50 at the commencement of the operation, the price of redemption would fluctuate from $16\frac{1}{2}$ to 25 years purchase, according to the rife of ftocks from 50 to 75. This is confidered as a fufficient inducement to the land owner to agree to the *propofal* in all its parts, as an extremely advantageous bargain in itfelf, exclufive of the urgency of the fituation, and the indifpenfable neceffity of recurring, under that fituation, to ftrong meafures. But care fhould be taken to confine this privilege to the land owners—and that it fhould not be *tranfferable*, as that would be depriving the public of the benefit arifing from the fale of what part is not redeemed: and for the fame reafon the exclufive privilege of redemption allowed to the land owner fhould be reftricted to a *limited time* *.

6th.

---

* But if this be confidered too great a facrifice to the land owner, and if the right of pre-emption at 25 years purchafe be deemed a fufficient advantage, the produce of the premium would be greater to the public, as in that cafe the land owner would pay the fame price as the other purchafers, and the premium would fluctuate, as defcribed in (14), according to the price of ftocks. But it muft be obferved that this, would, at the fame time, be taking away *the competition between the land owner and the ftock holder*, which is the part of the plan that has the moft direct tendency to raife the ftocks. The plan, under every poffible view of it, will be found to balance between the produce of the premium and raifing the ftocks. If the fum produced by the premium be very great, the rife will be proportionally lefs—and

6th. The price of land being at this time at 30 years purchafe, the land tax annuity is fairly worth the fame price. So that befides the great advantage to the land owner in allowing 75 for his *3 per cent.* ftock now under 50, he has here a farther advantage of five years purchafe, for which I fhall hereafter lay a claim to fome compenfation when I come to propofe the new taxes for the enfuing year.

7th. That failing of the land owners redeeming within the limited time, commiffioners fhould be appointed to fell the annuity to the beft advantage under fuch regulations as fhould be neceffary—as under every fuppofable price of ftock this annuity would fell for a premium, of which I fhall fpeak more fully hereafter.

It is to be remembered that the price in this cafe, as in the former of redemption by the land owner, is to be paid in *3 per cent.* ftock, valued to the purchafer at 75.

8th. That on the delivery of ftock by the redemptioner or purchafer, receipts fhould be iffued —but with fome mark of diftinction, as the latter

---

if the rife be great, the produce of the premium will be *proportionally* lefs: But, in either cafe, the advantage to the public is certain, and the fuccefs infallible. And in this circumftance I conceive that the merit of the plan principally confifts.

fhould be transferable at pleafure, and the former not before a limited time, four or five years, for example, for the reafon affigned in (5).

9th. That lifts of the redemptioners fhould be fent to the land tax collectors, and the receipt would be a difcharge from his land tax to that amount. If neceffity or convenience induced him to transfer it, after the time limited, notice muft be given to the land tax collectors to receive his land tax as before.

10th. From the nature and fecurity of this annuity; being, in effect, the firft mortgage on every eftate for only a fifth part of its *rated* value, under the fanction of government, it is clear that it would be the moft valuable transferable property in the kingdom, and would be eagerly bought up for family fettlements and arrangements. It would alfo be of great convenience in borrowing money in emergency; as the land owners, holding thefe receipts, would at all times poffefs the facility of raifing money.

11th. From the above it is clear, that the interefts of the land owner are amply provided for. I fhall proceed to ftate its effects to the public.

Two

Two millions a year, at 25 years purchafe, produce 50 millions, and 50 millions buy up 66,666,666⅔l. of 3 *per cent.* ftock, at 75; and as the intereft of 66,666,666⅔l. or two-thirds of 100 millions of 3 *per cent.* ftock, is two millions, it is clear that the public could, in no fuppofable cafe, be a lofer by the tranfaction; but that they would receive all the relative and collateral advantages of the meafure, which are of infinite confideration at this moment, without any facrifice: and that they would farther be gainers by whatever the 3 *per cents* may hereafter rife above 75, as well as by the *premium* on the fale of the annuity.

12th. It may, at firft fight, be imagined, that 75 is too high a price to take in 3 *per cents* at; and that, under the prefent circumftances, better terms might be infifted on for the public. If the whole 50 millions could be received at once, and employed in buying up 3 *per cent.* ftock, fome advantage might poffibly be derived thereby. But even this, if the fuppofition were practicable, would be very doubtful, from the great rife that fo prodigious a fum, brought at once into the ftock market, would infallibly produce. But at all events, this advantage would be much more than compenfated by taking in the ftock at 75; as, befides raifing the ftocks, which it has in common with the other, it prefents a plan, not only perfectly *practicable,* but holding out fo favourable terms

to

to the land owner, as to reconcile him to the meafure in all its parts; befides carrying in itfelf the certain means of 'execution, to whatever price the 3 *per cents* may rife. For,

13th. Four pounds of the land tax annuity at 25 years purchafe coft 100*l.* fterling, to be paid in 3 *per cent.* ftock, at 75, making·133⅓*l.* of 3 *per cent.* ftock, the intereft of which is likewife four pounds a year. So that if the 3 *per cents* were at 100*l.* the purchafer would ftill have the fame intereft, by exchanging 133⅓*l.* of his 3 *per cent.* ftock for four pounds of the land tax annuity, for which he would in reality pay only 25 years purchafe, according to the price of money, and value of ftock at the time : as the land tax annuity, being a 4 *per cent.* ftock, would follow the price of all the other ftocks, with the difference of the fuperior value arifing from the fecurity of the *mortgage,* which may, at the loweft, be computed at 5 *per cent.* and which holds good, whatever price ftocks may be at ; as this annuity will ftill poffefs that relative fuperiority, or bear a *premium* to that amount.

14th. It is not poffible to calculate what fum the *premium* on the fale of the land tax annuity would produce, as that depends on the price of ftocks at the time, and would fluctuate with them. But I can fay, that it ought invariably to be the
differ-

difference between the *actual price* of the 3 *per cent.* ſtocks, and 75, the *commutation price,* with 5 *per cent.* more for the *mortgage.* As for example: the man who ſhould buy 3 *per cent.* ſtock at 50, and pay 25*l.* in addition to every 100*l.* of his ſtock, would purchaſe the land tax annuity at 25 years purchaſe. If ſtocks roſe to 60, he ſhould pay the difference 15, and ſo on, excluſive of the 5 *per cent.* which I admit only to take place as the 3 *per cents* riſe to 75, which, in my opinion, this meaſure would infallibly produce; and for this purpoſe, a certain ſum, as 100,000*l.* a day, ſhould only be brought to market, to give time for the meaſure to have its full effect, and produce a gradual riſe. But it ſhould be kept in view, that as the ſtocks riſe, the premium will be leſs productive, and *vice verſá.*

15th. As ſupporting *public credit* is the great object of this meaſure, in preference even to pecuniary advantages, I conceive the great and incalculable advantages of it to conſiſt in raiſing the ſtocks, ſo as to enable the miniſter to make a loan; the withdrawing 66⅔ millions from the 3 *per cent.* ſtock, the effects of which would be immediately felt: and, above all, the preventing the frightful depreciation; which, without ſome ſuch meaſure, muſt neceſſarily reſult from the continuance of the war, and a new loan.

16th.

16th. But as it may be queftioned, whether this meafure will produce the effect I have ftated, of raifing the funds; I will take a view of its operation, under the moft unfavourable fuppofition that can be made, as that the 3 *per cents.* fhould continue at 50. In that cafe the premium on every 100*l.* ftock would be 25*l.* as I have fhown in (14), which, on the whole annuity, would produce the fum of 16 millions and two-thirds of a million fterling. If it fhould be deemed expedient to apply this fum to the fervice of the enfuing year, it muft be received by inftalments, for obvious reafons; but if taken in 3 *per cent.* ftock, 16 ⅔ millions fterling would liquidate 33 ⅓ millions, of 3 *per cent.* ftock at 50, making with 66⅔ millions, a total of 100 millions of 3 *per cent.* ftock received, or paid in, for the two millions land tax annuity; which would give a furplus of a million a year, to be applied towards the intereft of the new loan, in lieu of new taxes.

If the 3 *per cents* fhould rife to 60, the premium on the whole annuity would be ten millions, and fo on, in the fame proportion, to whatever price they may be at under 75; but if the price fhould rife above 75, the premium would ftill be 5 *per cent.* or 3¼ millions fterling (13). So that in whatever degree the price of ftocks fluctuates, a proportionate advantage will be found, either in the rife of ftocks, and the terms of the new loan; or in the produce of the premium.

But

But as a very great rife may be expected, the
new loan had better not be fettled for, until after
the rife; as otherwife, by contracting for it before
the rife, the public would lofe every way, for they
would, in effect, fell cheap and buy dear.

———————————

From the above ftatement I hope it is evident,
that the Propofal I have fubmitted is pregnant
with infinite advantages to the public profperity;
that it is perfectly practicable under every circumftance; and that, fo far from fhaking public credit, it would ftrengthen and confirm it.

These confiderations would alone be fufficient
to induce every judicious and difcerning land
owner, not only to agree to the *perpetuity*, which,
in reality, I confider to be no facrifice, with the
conditions above ftated; but alfo to go one ftep
farther, and to agree to a new tax of 6*d.* in the
pound on all revenue, generally: I mean on actual net rent of lands; of houfes above   *l.* a
year; church revenue above   *l.* a year; falaries
above   *l.* a year; ftock dividends, net profits of
canals, wharfs, docks, &c.

But I would recommend, that no attempt fhould
be made to extend this tax to profits on *agriculture,
manufactures, mines, fhipping, fifheries,* or *trade.*
The reafon is plainly this; on the firft clafs the

tax

tax would be paid only once by the individual af-
feffed; but in the fecond, the public would have
to pay it repeatedly; as the farmer, the miner, the
manufacturer, and the merchant, could charge it
one very article they furnifhed and fold, and thus
repay themfelves with intereft. Nor can this by
any regulation be prevented.

To reconcile the land owner to this tax, I would
beg of him to confider, that fome taxes muft be
impofed, and that it is perhaps impoffible, at this
day, to propofe taxes to half the amount only,
that would affect him fo little as a direct tax of 6d.
in the pound; for every fhilling taken by it out of
his pocket goes to the treafury; but if laid on
cuftoms or excife, the public pay generally ten
times as much as the treafury receives.

Befides, I beg him to underftand that this is
fpecifically the *compenfation* I laid claim to (6),
in lieu of the five years purchafe remitted in the
redemption price of the old land tax. Five years
purchafe of 4s. is equal to an annuity of 9¼d. and
one fifth of a penny computed at 25 years purchafe, if laid on as *rated;* in lieu of which I propofe an equalized tax of only 6d. in the pound on
actual profit rents; which I admit to be a little
addition, but which he will perceive is a very
flight one indeed.

C   But

But there is one cogent argument that applies to all the *Proprietors* I have named—that the people are heavily preffed already by the taxes; that they confider the war, as more particularly car.ied on for the protection of property, and that prudence and policy call on them to come forward, and take what remains of the burden on themfelves.

To the *church* this argument applies with ftill more peculiar force; for though I do not agree with Mr. Burke, " that this is a religious war," yet certainly religion is deeply interefted in the event; and I truft their own good fenfe and patriotic fpirit will anticipate the reafons that difcretion forbids me to detail.

To the *ftock holder* I fhould reprefent the equity of his contributing a little to fupport his all—the policy of his paying 6*d.* to infure a pound, and the prodigious profit he makes by the rife of ftocks in confequence of this meafure, which, if only 10 *per cent.* would be 133½ years of the propofed tax. Again, I confider a direct tax of 6*d.* in the pound of the dividend to be an eafier and pleafanter mode of contributing than by ftamps on transfers and receipts. Befides, as the benefit of this meafure is principally to fall on the ftock holders; they fhould invite the other Proprietors to join in the meafure, by coming forward

ward readily and cheerfully, and taking the lead by a voluntary offer.

Taking the land rental at 25 millions, and the ſtock dividends at 16¼, theſe two would produce upwards of a million a year ; and without having materials to make any calculation, I ſhould conjecture, that the remaining objects might raiſe half a million more.

This tax would unite the advantages of being certain, productive, eaſy in the collection, and not interfering with any other tax.

The only difficulty that any man would make to agreeing to ſo light a tax, would be from the apprehenſion of having it doubled the next year, if the war continued : and therefore, to remove this objection, I ſhould propoſe to ſatisfy him fully, as to this point, by now raiſing a fund of three millions a year, as a reſource for two years ſupplies, if the war ſhould ſo long continue. So great an exertion would confound the views of our enemies, who ſpeculate on exhauſting our reſources, and ſubduing us by expenſe.

Under theſe circumſtances, no trifling or doubtful objects ſhould be reſorted to : but the produce ſhould be certain, and the fund ſufficient. And, above all, care ſhould be taken that the public did

. not

not pay more than the treafury received. In the object I have in view, all thefe material circumftances are combined? and yet I am aware, that unfounded clamour would for a time be attempted to be raifed againft it, though every confideration of juftice and equity is in favour of its being adopted. The object I allude to is a more equalized duty on malt liquors. At prefent, the labourer in the country who earns a fhilling a day, cannot buy a quart of ale under 6d.; the London labourer who earns his 2s 6d and 3s a day, has his pot of porter (preferable as a nourifhing liquor) for $3\frac{1}{2}d$. Can any thing be fo unfairly regulated? If the prices were reverfed, there would be fome appearance of equity and fair play: but I repeat it, the prefent excife of malt liquors is iniquitous and oppreffive. If the price of both was fixed at 4d as it certainly might with advantage to the revenue, the London labourer would ftill have the advantage over the country labourer, by his higher wages, and more nourifhing liquor. One halfpenny a pot added on porter would produce about 650,000l. a year. But as fome regulation ought to be introduced to lower the price of beer and ale, which would fomewhat reduce the prefent revenue, I fhould allow the new duty to produce only 500,000l.

To the third and laft object I likewife forefee fome oppofition; as what refource can be propofed

at

at prefent, that is not liable to many difficulties and objections? But that muft be allowed to be the beft that is liable to the feweft, and therefore I would propofe to fupply from the *finking fund* what may be neceffary to make up the three millions, in cafe it fhould be wanted for the fecond year; and as fome compenfation, the furplus of the other new taxes over the fervice of the enfuing year might be applied to the finking fund. No man fets a higher value on the falutary effects of the finking fund than I do, as I confider it not only as the means of reducing the heavy weight of debt, but, what is of infinitely greater confequence, of correcting at a proper time, the whole fyftem of taxation, and of abolifhing thofe impofts whofe tendency is to raife the price of the neceffaries of life to the poor; for taxes being always impofed in times of difficulty and diftrefs, are rather the children of accident than reafon; and, in their prefent form, have more the appearance of a mafs of jarring atoms than the parts of a regular fyftem.

But as the finking fund is now upwards of four millions, the withdrawing 8 or 900,000*l* if wanted, would be better than the laying new taxes to that amount: and this deftruction from the finking fund would be in fome degree compenfated to it by the advantage it would receive by liquidating 66 ¾ millions of the 3 *per cents.* at 75, as in

two

two years after the peace there can fcarcely be a doubt that the confols will be at par.

As this may be fairly queftioned, I will give my reafons for thinking fo. On a peace, the draughts for money that has been locked up as the property of the ftates engaged in the war, muft be very confiderable ; and if not corrected by the intereft of the owners, which will lead them to wait for a rife, muft deprefs the ftocks for the firft two years : but that over, they cannnot fail to get up rapidly ; for the intereft of the national debt is, at prefent, about $16\frac{1}{4}$ millions, and the loan of the enfuing year will raife it probably to $17\frac{1}{4}$, of which fum, as monied men always give a pre- ference to the funds, we may fairly compute, that nearly a half, or eight millions a year, will be in- vefted, while ftocks are low. Add to this four millions from the finking fund, and it will form a mafs of 12 millions, that we may admit will be employed in buying ftock and raifing the funds, independent of the favings of individuals and pro- fits that may be laid out in the fame way : for the greater the debt, and the greater the intereft, the more rapidly will the ftocks be raifed after the peace. Though this may at firft view appear a little paradoxical, yet in reality nothing is more true, owing to the great increafe of the funds em- ployed in purchafing : and fo far from thinking this an advantage, I confider it a difadvantage,

as

as it counteracts the operation of the finking fund, to the prejudice of the public, and profit of individuals. ·

The ſtocks have generally been called the *pulſe* of the nation; and purſuing this metaphor, I ſhould ſay, that I conſider the 3 *per cents* at 75 as the pulſe of health, ſtrength, and vigour—that all above is feveriſh heat; all below, tending to weakneſs and debility. I have already ſaid, that this *Propoſal*, if adopted, will have the tendency to raiſe the conſols to 75 ; if it were poſſible to diſcover any meaſure that could have a ſimilar tendency to prevent their riſing above 75, it would be diſcovering the moſt valuable ſecret in finance. If it be admitted that the principle is right, I ſhould not deſpair of human ingenuity making great improvements in the ſyſtem of finance, which has been hitherto rather practiſed as a trade, than ſtudied as a ſcience. If 75 be admitted as a central point, I apprehend it may furniſh valuable hints to direct the application of the finking fund to the two great objects, of *reducing the debt*, and *aboliſhing taxes*. While the conſols are under 75, the finking fund ſhould be employed to buy up ſtock; when they riſe above 75, it would be of more public utility to aboliſh taxes than to purchaſe ſtock: and in this manner, by judicious management, the price of proviſions and neceſſaries would be gradually lowered, and things

C 4　　　　brought

brought back to a better ſtate, without convulſion, which generally attends ſudden change.

Many ingenious writers have pointed out the
injurious effects of the abuſe of *paper money;*
but I do not recollect that any of them have
pointed out the means of correcting the abuſe, or
even of diſcovering at what point the abuſe be-
gan. I would beg leave to ſubmit to their conſi-
deration, whether the latter may not be found
from the price of the ſtocks; and if this be re-
cogniſed, it would not be imparcticable to point
out the means of, in ſome degree, correcting the
abuſe, without injury to uſeful improvement, or
even rational ſpeculation. But as I mean only
to throw out hints on theſe ſubjects, without en-
tering on a diſcuſſion which requires abilities far
ſuperior to mine, I ſhall be happy to ſee them
treated by abler hands.

I ſhall now briefly advert to an obſervation
made before, that the national debt is *the ſource
of ſupplies;* as; in order to guard againſt the miſ-
conſtructions that it may be liable to, I think it ne-
ceſſary to explain myſelf a little more at large on
this ſubject, and then I ſhall conclude.

The national debt is evidently a great *accumulation* of wealth, formed either from the ſavings
and profits of our own nation, or from capital remitted by foreigners and lent to the ſtate; for the
ſe

ufe of which the public pay an intereft. If the
land produce 25 millions a year, and the national
debt upwards of 16; to the land owner and the
ftock holder it is indifferent from what fources their
income is drawn—confidered fimply as *income*,
they ftand on precifely the fame footing: but here
the parallel ends, as they differ in every other refpect. The land revenue arifes from the produc-
tion of articles of confumption—the debt revenue from funds invefted and employed in agriculture, manufactures, commerce, &c. &c. The
whole, or nearly the whole of the land revenue is
again fpent in *confumption*—by far the greater
part of the debt revenue is converted into *new
capital*. To this capital we are indebted for all
the great improvements we every where fee around
us; but particularly in this immenfe city, round
which it has reared beautiful towns in every di-
rection. This capital has fought occupation in
every corner of the kingdom, and pufhed enter-
prife through every quarter of the globe. It has
improved and extended agriculture, manufactures,
and commerce: it has eftablifhed fifheries, funk
mines, dug canals, built cities, and beautified the
country,—and to fum up all, it has furnifhed fupplies for the prefent expenfive war to an amount
beyond the bounds of all previous calculation,
and fcarce credible even after the event. So that
the French have been completely difappointed
in calculating on the ruin of our refources from

our

expenfive exertions, as we were by fallacious rea-
fonings on the overthrow of the French government from the depreciation of their affignats. In
fpite of the great expence, Great Britain flou-
rifhes ; the affignats have difappeared, but the
republic remains.

In fact, every year that adds to the debt, adds a
new fund for the fervice of the next—and we
fhould find no difficulty in raifing the fupplies for
any length of time to which the war may be pro-
longed, if we can equally find the means to pay
the intereft. I have already fhown the eafy and
certain means of raifing a fund of three millions a
year without diftrefs or inconvenience ; and other
ways equally unobjectionable may be devifed.
But to prevent all doubt or cavil on the fubject,
the finking fund, if it were *abfolutely* neceffary to
divert it from its prefent object, prefents the certain refource of three millions more, making in
all upwards of *fix millions*, which the ftate has at
command, without laying a fingle fhilling on induftry or trade.

The French, by protracting the war in the hope
of ruining our finances, are entailing all the hor-
rors of an unfettled and diforderly ftate on their
own fubjects ; and by the example of their increafing inteftine diftractions, holding out an in-
ftructive leffon to all Europe, to avoid plunging
into the chaos of revolution. France indeed has,

hitherto

hitherto, derived great refources from plunder and the contributions raifed from the conquered pro-vinces : but money thus produced, like the gold imported into Spain from the mines of America, flows out immediately, without enriching the country through which it has paffed. Nor would the wealth of Europe, if circulated in this man-ner through France, as a tube of conveyance, have any effect in enriching the ftate. This can only be done by induftry and the arts of peace ; and when fhe has exhaufted herfelf by ineffectual ftruggles, fhe will return from the delufion, ex-haufted and difappointed ; and I am inclined to think, from a variety of circumftances, that this period is not far diftant, The good fenfe of a high-fpirited people cannot be much longer im-pofed on. They muft fee that they are dupes to the ambition of their rulers : that they are living under a more arbitrary defpotifm than that which they abolifhed ; and that the people have loft in property, whatever the members and engines of the revolutionary fyftem have gained. It is as much the intereft of the people to put an end to the war, as it is of their executive to continue the fyftem of diforder with which it is connected. The fenfe of the people was articulately expreffed on this fubject in the proceedings antecedent to the 4th of September; and though the public voice has been fuppreffed by violence, it cannot be fo long.

By

By the recent peace with the Emperor, even the precarious refource of plunder and exaꞓtion is cut off; and the French armies, if kept up, muſt now derive their ſupport from the internal reſources of confiſcation, or from the forced contributions of their allies. Accordingly, an attempt was lately made, by the partiſans of the Directory, to ſeize at one blow on the property of the whole claſs of the nobility; but it was too monſtrous to be adopted by the councils; and thus diſappointed at home, they will probably turn their views towards their allies. They have the mines of South America on the one ſide, and the bank of Amſterdam on the other; and Charles Delacroix's miſſion will ſoon appear to have another objeꞓt than that of ſettling the Dutch conſtitution.

I have, I hope, ſatisfaꞓtorily ſhown, that the expenditure of every year is converted into a fund for the next, and inſtead of leſſening increaſes our means: for no diminution is made to the national wealth by the immenſe ſums annually ſpent by government, inaſmuch as government is no more than a *cuſtomer* trading to an immenſe amount, and annually adding a great accumulation to the monied capital of the kingdom. If the government expenſes exhauſted the wealth of the kingdom, it is ſelf-evident that thoſe expenſes never could have exceeded the ſum total of that wealth— if wealth be conſidered as money: but ſo far is this

from

from being the cafe, that the expenfes of the laft year, or the fum received by the exchequer, amounted to nearly three times the fum total of all the circulating money, both paper and coin, in the kingdom.

This is a phenomenon that lays all fyftems in the duft, and will be a fertile fubject for future difcuffion to political writers; but I fhall content myfelf with fimply ftating the facts—It had ever been a doubt to what amount the paper currency of the bank of England had been iffued; public opinion had generally rated it from 30 to 40 millions; but when the books of the bank were laft winter laid before Parliament, it appeared, to the aftonifhment of all mankind, that it did not amount to nine millions. The only mode of efti-mating the circulating paper of all the *country banks* is by a comparifon with the bank of Eng-land; and as they had all confiderably narrowed their iffue of paper on the breaking out of the war, I think it could not laft year have amounted to fix millions—and as the gold coin had been locked up in the bank of England, and in all the private banks, befides the quantities hoarded by individuals, it appears to me that the gold and filver coin remaining in circulation could not amount to five millions, making in paper and coin a capital of 20 millions.

Let

Let us now take a view of the expenfes of government. In the firft place, the produce of the taxes
and the ordinary revenue amounted to upwards of
20 millions—the two loans to $32\frac{1}{2}$—and the exchequer bills to $3\frac{1}{4}$ millions—making in all upwards of 56 millions, or nearly three times the
circulating money of the kingdom; and yet the
whole of this enormous fum either has been paid,
or will be by Chriftmas, into the exchequer; and
that without deranging the other money tranfac-
tions, which have all held their ordinary courfe.
The land rents, houfe rents, &c. &c. have been
paid; the church, the law, and phyfic have received their ufual ftipends. Manufactures have
been carried on, and trade has flourifhed without
fhock or interruption. I confider the total revenue
of the kingdom to exceed 100 millions; and the
whole of this revenue has been collected, together
with upwards of 58 millions raifed for government,
by the means of only about 20 millions of circulating money—at a time too that the withdrawing
the gold coin from circulation had certainly weak-
ened confidence, if it did not fhake public credit.

Here is a feries of facts that confound all previous reafoning on our refources and means. We
may take an infinite variety of views from thefe
facts; but from the number of circumftances that
enter into the confideration, I look upon it as impoffible to give any other account of fo aftonifhing

ing effects, than that they are all produced by
circulation: but whether circulation be the cause
or the effect, or both combined; in what manner
so many interests move in their different orbits,
balanced by one another, and all contributing to
the beauty and strength of the general system, we
can no more say; than we can comprehend the
ultimate cause of the revolutionary motions of the
heavenly bodies.

I am not surprised that men have been mistaken
in conjectures on a subject where every thing is
new, in many parts contrary to established ideas,
and where history and experience furnish no materials to argue from. The very enemy who have
speculated on the ruin of our finance, have con-
tributed greatly to the success and support of our
funded system, unintentionally I allow, but not
the less certainly; for the general derangement of
the money capitals in their own republic, as well
as through a great part of Germany and Italy,
adjoining to France, has forced the wealth of
those countries to fly for security to Great Britain,
as the only place of refuge from rapine and violence; for money cannot be confined or restrained.
- By means of bills of exchange, it travels, unseen,
from one end of Europe to the other; and eludes
the jealousy of the *tyrant* and the grasp of the
despot.

I have

I have heard it faid, that it was a favourite object of the French government to deftroy our
funded fyftem. I can fcarce believe that they are
fo ignorant of the nature of finance, as not to
know that there is one general fyftem of finance
extending over Europe—that money flows freely,
and circulates like water; that though, from the
circumftances of the prefent war, and the fyftem
of terror, plunder, and confifcation, acting as a
barrier, or *dyke*; a vaft accumulation has been
formed in our funds; yet the moment that this
dyke is removed, and money feels itfelf fecure in
France and on the continent, it will immediately
flow back on thofe countries, until it again return
to its proper level. So that, if they could fuc-
ceed in deftroying our funds, they would deftroy
the means of their own future happinefs, and
dry up the fources which they ought to look to,
in order to refrefh their wafted country, and reftore
arts, manufactures, and commerce, to their former flourifhing ftate. We are the bankers of
Europe, and it is their intereft perhaps more than
ours, that we fhould not become bankrupts.

M. Necker and Monfieur de Calonne, who
differed in fo many other points, agreed in this,
that the circulating coin of the kingdom of
France, before the revolution, amounted to between 90 and 96 millions of our money; and yet
neither the abilities of the one, nor the addrefs of
the

the other, could raife the revenue to 26 millions; nor has the republican government ever in one year raifed this fum in the courfe of regular reve- nue, exclufive of the produce of public property, and the fpoils of confifcation. And the reafon is the fame in both cafes, arifing from the nature of the government, which being founded in de- fpotifm, and not poffeffing public confidence, is deprived of the means which a popular govern- ment, founded in *good faith* and the *protection* of *property*, enjoys. The republic has been hitherto more arbitrary than the monarchy, as no tyranny can be equal to that of a *revolutionary fyftem*— and fo far has property been from receiving fecu- rity from a change of government, that it has experienced additional violence and injuftice.

It is aftonifhing that the example of Great Britain fhould not have taught this ufeful leffon to all the ftates of Europe, that nothing can enrich a ftate, and attraft property, but fecurity and pro- teftion; and that thefe can only be found in a fteady, popular government, with juft laws, and an impartial adminiftration of juftice.—Abfolute governments extort money by force; Great Bri- tain raifes it, not only from her own people, but from all the world; and the fubjefts of her ene- mies are the foremoft in offering their contribu- tions. Abfolute governments, in raifing fupplies, aft by the *fcrew*; popular governments, by the

D

com-

combined powers of the *lever* and the *pulley*. We have erected our machinery on the folid rock of *good faith* and *public credit*; and have there found the ground that Archimedes required.

If France had founded her revolution on the *protection* of *property*, inftead of the principles of *plunder* and *diforganization*, fhe might have become the envy of Europe, and made the happi- nefs of her own people, by occupying them in the arts of peace and domeftic happinefs; inftead of wafting their blood in ufelefs conquefts.

The French government have broken off two negociations for peace, begun, the one at Paris, and the other at Lifle, on the fame pretence, that our ambaffador had not fufficient powers to treat. The firft was opened on the principle of *mutual com- penfation:* but the principle was no fooner ad- mitted, than it was loft fight of; and our ambaffa- dor, as if bewildered in the mazes of detail, dropt the *thread*, that would have conducted him fafely through the labyrinth. A new bafis was ftarted by the French minifter, founded on *their* conftitution, and exifting treaties—a pretenfion which it is not eafy to fay, whether more arrogant or abfurd; it was, in effect, prefcribing the law, and dictating terms as to a conquered province: and the only furprife is, not that a fecond negociation fhould have been broken off on fo frivolous a pretence, but

but that a fecond fhould have been opened, without a fpecific renunciation of fo infolent a pretenfion. What has Great Britain to do with the interior decrees and conftitutions of France, or with her fecret engagements contracted with *her* friends, and *our* enemies? Such an affumption precludes the poffibility of treating, and abolifhes the idea of negociation. The French convention had decreed, that their dominions all over the world were conftituent parts of their new republic; and, again, that the Rhine fhould be their boundary on the fide of Germany:—that is, that they fhould retain all their conquefts within the Rhine, and that we fhould reftore all ours. They prefcribed the *uti poffidetis*, as the bafis in treating with the Emperor, and the *ftatus quo* in treating with us; and this they call mutual compenfation.

If their decrees are to be admitted as firft principles, they may vote Great Britain to be a conftituent part of their republic; and the abfurdity in the one cafe would not be greater than in the other.

That the Spaniards and Dutch, who have been dragooned into the war, fhould call upon the French for the performance of their engagements, is not to be wondered at; but while they fee that the French will make no *compenfation* for the conquefts we have made from them, they muft feel

that

that the French are not hearty in the bufinefs, or do not expe& a compliance with demands fo very unreafonable : and that their obje& is not to obtain a reftitution for them, but to involve them ftill deeper in the ruinous conne&ion which they have thruft upon them *.

The condu& of the French to their allies, the Spaniards and the Dutch, has, in variou> inftances, the appearance of jealoufy and diftruft; as if fenfible that they muft, fooner or later, break loofe from the fubje&ion they hold them in, and return to their natural alliance and connexion with Great Britain. On this principle we can only explain their expofing *their* fleets, while they keep their *own* inglorioufly, but fafely, laid up in port; their infolent memorial, delivered laft fummer to the court of Madrid, upbraiding the ina&ivity and cowardice of the Spanifh fleet in terms never ufed before by the *higheft* nation, nor fubmitted to by the *meaneft.;* and, laftly, the peremptory order given to De Winter, to proceed to fea and rifk an engagement, after his remonftrances on the confequences that muft refult from fo rafh and improvident a meafure. But the French may fay with Iago,

——Whether he kill Caffio,
Or Caffio him ; or each do kill the other,
Every way makes my gain.

* The above obfervations were written before his Majefty's Declaration appeared, and a fingle word has not been altered fince.

Having

Having thus enlarged more than I had original-
ly intended on the one fide of the picture, the ftate
of our refources for continuing the war, though I
have but barely touched on many fubjects that
deferve a more minute confideration ; I proceed
to make a few obfervations on the other fide, that
I may not be accufed of advancing abfurdities ; as
if I in any degree countenanced the idea, that our
refources were without limits, and that we might
proceed with funding *ad infinitum.* But thefe limits are to be found only in our powers to pay
the price or intereft ; for money would not be want-
ing. On this point, I have not refted general af-
fertion on vague fuppofition ; I have detailed the
refources to the amount I have fpecified, and I
pledge myfelf to nothing more. As the early
writers on the national debt have generally been
miftaken in their reafoning, and deductions, on
this fubject ; I will not venture any on events
which are dependent on a variety of circumftances
that cannot be forefeen.

The writers I allude to, have predicted that the
nation would be impoverifhed by the accumulation of debt :—I fay, it has been *enriched.*—They,
that the debt would confume the wealth and vi-
tals of the ftate ; whereas it has, in reality, produced an *excefs* of wealth. If the ftate ever pe-
rifh from this circumftance, it will not be fre
inanition, but from *repletion ;* it will die of a

thora, and not of an *atrophy.* We may, almoft without a metaphor, be faid to have realized the fable of Midas, whofe touch turned every thing into gold, and who. died of hunger, furrounded by a variety of food, converted into that precious metal by his eager grafp. Fifh, flefh, and fowl, have long been converted to the labouring claffes of our people; and even bread, to a portion of them, at times. This *tranfmuting* quality is by degrees creeping on to the middle ranks of life, and its effects are truly alarming. The *rife of price,* then, is the great evil refulting from our national debt, as affecting the poor, by the difficulty of procuring fubfiftence, and the middle ranks, by depriving them of comforts. The price of labour muft, in confequence, be augmented, which muft raife the price of our manufactures, and hurt their competition at foreign markets, or re-reduce the profits, until the manufacture muft be given up as a lofing bufinefs; and this would throw the hands, formerly employed in that branch, on the public for fubfiftence; which, again, would aggravate the evil.

Other caufes may combine to enhance price; but they will all be found to refolve themfelves into the great operating caufe, the increafe of revenue, or money, arifing from the immenfe accumulation of our funded fyftem. Thofe who deal in money, float on the furface, and rife with the

tide

tide ; to them the increafe of price is more than compenfated by the increafe of income ; but all thofe whofe income is fixed, as landlords, labourers, clerks, churchmen, people retired from bufinefs and living on a capital, foldiers, failors, &c. &c. are in danger of being buried under the inundation.

Every man complains of the expenfe of living being nearly doubled within the laft twenty years; and the public have an incontrovertible and melancholy proof of it, in the expenditure of the prefent war. Without going further back than the laft two reigns, we have feen the annual expenfe of our war eftablifhment rife from five to ten millions ; from ten to twenty ; and the prefent year, if fully provided for, would have been little fhort of forty millions. Is it impoffible to proceed in this career? I forbear the anfwer. But it is certainly, and clearly, the intereft of every minifter, and public man, to exert every means to check the progrefs, and to bring things back to a *more moderate*, and *better poifed*, fyftem.

I fhall hereafter mention fome of the inferior caufes that have a tendency to raife price ; but the great efficient caufe is the prodigious increafe of wealth, and the rapid accumulation of our funded fyftem. In the courfe of four years upwards of fix millions a year have been added to

the

the public revenue, or to the fund deftined to purchafe articles of confumption ; and as the no-minal price of provifions muft depend on the quantity, compared with the quantity of money; and as little or no addition has, in that period, been made to the ftock of provifions, it is eafy to fee how the price muft be enhanced by the great increafe of revenue. The fuddennefs of this great increafe has, probably, forced price to a higher point, than it will fettle to hereafter ; and the great demand for government from the enormous, and unheard-of, expenditure of the two laft years.

I muft here beg leave to obferve, that of all the poffible means that human wifdom can point out, for counteracting this evil, the moft certain and operative is one which is otherwife connected with the happinefs, population, and profperity of the nation, in every refpect ; and that is, the improv-ing and extending agriculture, and encouraging every art for increafing the ftock of *animal* and *vegetable food*: for every addition to the produce of the earth will directly in that proportion coun-terbalance the inconveniences arifing from the ac-cumulation of national debt; as they all arife not from the *fum*, but from the *difproportion* intro-duced between circulating revenue and articles of confumption. While the war continues, the ex-cefs of money revenue will be in great part converted

verted into new capital, to fupply refources : but
in time of peace this excefs would find its beft
employment, in furnifhing an antidote to itfelf in
the improvement and extenfion of agriculture.

I beg leave farther to obferve, that taxation, in
its quality of taking money out of the pockets of
the people, has a direct tendency to lower price,
and not to raife it ; and if the money thus received
were withdrawn entirely from circulation, this
would be the cafe: but, inftead of this, it is collected from thoufands of hands and in millions of
ways, and accumulated into an immenfe mafs,
which, being again difcharged in large fums, ac-
quire an increafed force from the magnitude and
velocity with which they act on confumable com-
modities. If the waters of a thoufand fprings,
ftreams, and rivulets, that would have quietly
and gently flowed through the country, were to be
collected into an immenfe *refervoir*, and let loofe
at ftated periods ; their force and velocity would
give us an adequate idea of the effects produced
by the accumulation of money formed from taxation.

There are other caufes befides the increafe of
money, that have a direct tendency to raife the
price of provifions ; as the great demand for our
fleets and armies, the wafte of ftores during the
war, and injudicious taxes, which, in certain inftances,

ftances, raife price beyond all proportion to their actual produce. For this reafon, direct taxes, whenever they can be found productive, are infinitely preferable to indirect taxes; which, unluckily, from being lefs perceived, and left at the option of the perfon who pays them, have been lefs the object of complaint.

By direct taxes, I mean fuch as the land tax, commutation tax, taxes on coaches, horfes, fervants, hats, gloves, &c. &c. which are paid once and no more. By indirect taxes, I underftand fuch cuftom and excife duties as become a part of the price of the article ; and on which, blended with the prime coft, every perfon through whofe hands they pafs to the confumer, exacts a profit. But even a direct tax may be objectionable, if laid on an improper object, of which we have an inftance in the tax laid on cart horfes and horfes employed in farming. The minifter was right in thinking that farming profits could bear the duty; but the farmer poffeffes the facility of charging the duty on every bufhel of corn or load of hay, on every bullock or fheep, nay, on every pound of butter fent to market; and thus repaying himfelf with intereft. The fame objection lay againft the turnpike duty propofed laft year, but judicioufly given up.

There

There are inftances, however, of indirect taxes being preferable to direct taxes, of which I fhall give an inftance in the ftamp duty on gold and the duty on gold watches. The ftamp on gold produced between 2 and 3l. on a gold watch, which was not perceived or complained of, but the direct tax of half a guinea on a gold watch has induced great numbers to change their gold cafes for metal; and if the fafhion becomes general, the exchequer will lofe by the additional duty.

To return to my fubject: I have, I truft, faid enough to fhew that I feel the neceffity of reducing the national debt, founded on reafons arifing from our internal fituation; without admitting the gloomy predictions drawn from the relative fituation of the continent and the price of living, as prefenting irrefiftible temptations to our manufacturers to emigrate. [But I would not pafs the matter over in filence, as afraid to meet it; for I do not join in the apprehenfions entertained on this fubject, when I know that Ireland has at all times poffeffed fuperior inducements to what France can offer to our manufacturers, as a more temperate climate than England, and a richer foil: the fame language, manners, and laws; cheap living, low taxes, neither poor rates nor land tax; navigable rivers and canals, and the fineft harbours in Europe, advantageoufly fituated for foreign trade: and yet, with all thefe

advantages,

advantages, Ireland has never been able to draw the Englifh manufacturer from his fettlement; nor the merchant from the eftablifhed courfe of his trade.

I will not now ftop to enquire what other mea-fures may be adopted, on a peace, to reduce our debt and our taxes ; becaufe a change of circum-ftances may alter the effect of what would appear proper at prefent : but when the time arrives, our fituation will probably offer ample means to be employed for that purpofe, if no unlooked-for difafter happen, in the mean time, to counteract the view I have given of our affairs. But even then great difficulties will occur ; and great judg-ment will be requifite to guide the ftate machine down hill, and to retrace the fteps by which we have rifen to the giddy height of our funded fyf-tem. Neither would I venture to fay, that the fall of price will immediately follow the reduction of debt; as habit and cuftom will keep it up for fome time after the caufe has fubfided.

The reduction of our national debt is undoubt-edly a primary and moft important object ; and as a leading feature of the meafures to be purfued for attaining that object, I have ventured to fub-mit the above *Propofal*, being ftrongly impreffed with the great advantages that the public would derive from its being adopted at this moment ;

but

but without prefuming to think that it is perfect,
or even the beft that may be fuggefted. I fhall
be happy if it lead to farther examination and in-
inquiry, and pave the way for others to correct,
amend, and improve. As the object is great, the
very purfuit is praifeworthy, whether fuccefsful
or not ; and if any thing I have faid fhould induce
men of greater abilities to purfue the fubject, I
have the fatisfaction to think, that they will neither find falfe reafoning to embarrafs, nor mifre-
prefentation to perplex their courfe, as it has
been my fteady purpofe to purfue truth; unbiaffed
by partial views, uninfluenced by private friend-
fhip or party fpirit. The meafure I propofe is a
great national object, in the fuccefs of which the
fupporters of minifters and the friends of oppofition are equally interefted ; and as fuch, I recommend it to their impartial confideration.

F I N I S.

APPENDIX.

THE above PROPOSAL was written in the month of October, and shewn to some men of superior abilities, who thought favourably of it, and recommended the publication. It was accordingly sent to the press, much about the time that the Chancellor of the Exchequer brought forward his plan of finance; and as I foresaw that so great and novel a measure could not fail, for a time, to engross entirely the public attention, I withdrew my *proposal* from publication, until that measure should be in some way disposed of.

As the bill is now in nearly its last stage through the House of Commons, I have been prevailed on, by the renewed application from men, in whose judgement I place great confidence, to submit the above *proposal* to the public; requesting that it may be weighed dispassionately, and examined attentively, as containing a plan of the first importance to the *security of public credit*, and the *future happiness* and *prosperity* of the *state*.

As the above *proposal* was written before the assessed taxes were brought forward, it may be expected that I should shew, whether the *proposal* is affected by that measure, and in what manner; and that I should point out their bearings and relations to one another.

Without

Without going minutely into a bufinefs, which has been fo fully difcuffed, I fhall content myfelf, with making two obfervations, which will contain a fatisfactory explanation on the points required

1ft. That if the meafure I recommend in the *propofal* had been adopted, it would have rendered the other unneceffary ; as it prefents, I will venture to fay, a certain plan for raifing the fupply under 5 per cent. with great concomitant advantages to the public ; or of producing a fum of from 10 to $16\frac{1}{3}$ millions in diminution of the loan. And if now adopted, it would ftill produce the fame effects.

With this conviction on my mind, it is impoffible that I can approve of the new affeffment, as a *meafure of finance*, as from what I have faid above, it muft be clear that I do not think the public able to bear fo great an addition to their exifting burdens. From the manner in which the new affeffment is laid, there is reafon to expect that it will be productive ; but there is no lefs reafon to apprehend its creating a deficiency in the ordinary revenue, with various other inconveniences, which I fhould be difpofed to confider more at length, if I did not wifh to avoid the appearance of crying down the one with a view to raife the other ; and that I am fatisfied to reft the fuccefs of my *propofal* on its own proper merit on general grounds, without reference to any other.

I fhall only obferve that if, on more mature confideration, the bill fhould ftill be ftopped, the *propofal* I offer to the public, prefents a certain and unobjectionable plan for raifing the fupply in a manner that could not fail to be received with general approbation.

2d. That, though the plan I recommend would not, now, be productive of all the advantages that might have been derived from it, if carried into execution previous to the additional affeffment; yet it will ftill produce all the other great benefits of *raifing the ftocks, fupporting public credit*, and *reducing the national debt*. And the reafons derived from thefe confiderations remain equally cogent as they were before that meafure was thought of.

if

If it is afked, whether the new affeffment
pediment to the exccution of the plan I p
land owners of their ready-money, &c. I an
edly would to a certain degree, if the land
only purchafers, or if the price were to b
be afterwards ápplied to buy up ftock, as
prefent. But in order to keep clear of a
arife from the circumftances of the mon
during the operation, I purpofely laid it d
the purchafe fhould be paid in 3 *per cent.* ft
premium might be paid in the fame manne
purchafer. So that the only way in which
could affeĉt the execution of the *plan* would
competition between the land owner and th
I have ftated (5) to be the feature that had
dency to raife the price of ftocks.

I fhall conclude by obferving, that *this*
confideration of thofe men, who entertain
of the new affeffment, and apprehenfions of
who, notwithftanding, deem it dangerous
moment; as being impreffed with the abfo
viding for the public expence, and feeing
one propofed by the Chancellor of the Exch

To the Chancellor of the Exchequer h
at ftake on the fuccefs of the affeffment tha
and who, as truftee for the public revenue, n
diately affeĉted by a deficiency or derange
finance, this *Propofal* cannot be unacceptable;
that may be fubftituted in the room of the o
tive, unobjeĉtionable in every part, and *praĉica*
ftances.

December 25th, 1797.

F I N I S.

www.ingramcontent.com/pod-product-compliance
Lightning Source LLC
Chambersburg PA
CBHW031806090426
42739CB00008B/1184